Classic Songs of the 20s

Project Managers: Tony Esposito & Carol Cuellar

Text By: Fucini Productions, Inc.

Cover Design: Joseph Klucar

Art Layout: Martha L. Ramirez

Production Coordinator: Donna Salzburg

Contents

INTRODUCTION

Think big . . . Live fast . . . Make a splash. That was the credo of the Roaring '20s, a time of bright lights, speakeasies, brassy jazz, and unlimited confidence. Fresh from its victory over the Kaiser in "the war to end all wars," America rushed breathlessly into the future.

No dream was too big or too outlandish in the America of the '20s, when a booming bull market turned ordinary people into overnight millionaires on Wall Street; when a new technological wonder called radio was bringing music into everyone's living room; and when handsome young Charles Lindbergh became the first international superstar by flying a small plane across the dark skies over the Atlantic.

In arts, entertainment, fashion, literature, sports—and almost every other area of human endeavor—Americans were boldly challenging long-established conventions . . . and turning tradition on its head! Hemlines, which were just over the ankle in 1920, went up to scandalous heights, reaching above the knee by the end of the decade. Young "flappers" shocked their mothers by wearing rouge, bobbing their hair, and staying out all night, "packed tight as sardines," on dance floors doing the Charleston.

It wasn't only the young who were seeking good times and new experiences in the '20s. Weary of the sacrifices required of them during World War I, Americans of all ages were ready to cut loose and enjoy themselves playing the hot new card game, Mah Jong, taking up the growing sport of golf, or visiting that most famous '20s creation—the speakeasy. Is it any wonder that the most celebrated American hero of the decade was Babe Ruth, a larger-than-life figure known almost as much for his excesses as his colossal home runs?

Music not only reflects the changes that reshaped American society during the '20s, but it also helped define the unique character of this wonderfully brash and free-spirited decade. The saxophone, with its confident and powerful voice, blew past the more sedate violin to occupy center stage in the world of music. Propelled by the driving intensity of the saxophone, popular music captured the spontaneous spirit of a time when rules were changing fast and anything seemed possible.

So go ahead and enjoy this musical look back at the 1920s. We think you'll agree that it was one of the most exciting decades ever, both in spirit and song.

THE JAZZ AGE

The '20s moved to the rhythm of the jazz band. If jazz didn't exist before this decade began, the freewheeling tempo of the '20s would have inspired some musical genius somewhere to "invent" it. But jazz was already a rich and well-developed musical form in 1920, flourishing in the African-American community of New Orleans.

With its freedom from convention and its inspired distortions of musical tradition, jazz fit perfectly into the cultural climate of the '20s. From New Orleans, jazz traveled up the Mississippi like a heat wave rolling into St. Louis. Then, after a stopover in Kansas City, the Jazz Front moved east to Chicago and New York, picking up new creative energy along the way.

Many great jazzmen helped define jazz in the '20s, but few were as influential in spreading the joy of this musical genre as Fats Waller and Louis Armstrong.

Widely celebrated as a pianist and singer, Waller brought the sound of jazz to Broadway with his shows *Keep Shufflin'* and the ground-breaking hit *Hot Chocolate.* A spectacular showcase of African-American music, *Hot Chocolate* drew rave reviews and large crowds. For many white Americans, Waller's musical was their first exposure to serious black culture.

The most famous song in *Hot Chocolate,* and the composition that best captures the voice of Fats Waller in the '20s, is "Ain't Misbehavin'." Americans of all racial and cultural backgrounds responded to this Waller composition, making it one of the most frequently performed songs of the '20s.

Among the many jazz artists who recorded "Ain't Misbehavin'" was Louis Armstrong. In fact, the great Satchmo's version of this song was even more popular than Waller's original rendition. Born in New Orleans at the start of the twentieth century, Armstrong didn't pick up an instrument until his early teens, when his mentor, noted jazzman Joe Oliver, gave him a cornet.

Despite his youth and inexperience, Armstrong quickly became the brightest star of the Jazz Age, a glittering brilliant light of showmanship and joyous improvisation. In 1922, he performed with the Creole Jazz band at the Lincoln Gardens in Chicago, giving the Windy City its first real taste of New Orleans-style jazz. It was a case of "love at first listen." Chicagoans quickly embraced Armstrong and his powerful playing style, and the city became the center of the jazz universe during the '20s.

Shortly after arriving in Chicago, Armstrong switched from the cornet to the trumpet, an instrument better suited to the clear, bright sound that his musical vision demanded. Like America of the '20s, Armstrong was bold and daring—and eager to push into the unknown. Let Lindbergh fly the uncharted skies over the Atlantic; Louis Armstrong would navigate the tricky waters of improvisation and redefine the idea of the jazz solo. Let Babe Ruth rewrite the record book in baseball; Armstrong would build great solos and extend the trumpet range to a high F.

Armstrong's performances of songs like "If I Could Be With You (One Hour Tonight)" were instantly recognizable to black and white music lovers of the '20s. He dazzled audiences and inspired other jazz musicians with his clear articulation and the varied vibratos he used to color and embellish individual notes. For good measure, Armstrong also used his voice as a moving and seductive instrument, pioneering a style of "scat singing" that would greatly influence future jazz greats like Ella Fitzgerald.

It took a big, ebullient, and wildly confident style of music to keep pace with the Roaring '20s, and jazz artists like Fats Waller and Louis Armstrong provided this in a fashion that reflected the best of this remarkable decade.

Music in the Air (And on the Airwaves)

Music reached more people in the '20s than at any other time in the past. The reason can be summed up in a single word—*radio.* On November 2, 1920, KDKA in East Pittsburgh, Pennsylvania, became the world's first commercial radio station. It broadcast the results of the Harding-Cox presidential election. Politics soon gave way to music, and the sweet crooning of stars like Rudy Vallee

("Lover Come Back to Me") and the symphonic jazz sounds of Ben Bernie ("Sweet Georgia Brown") and Nat Shilkret ("One Kiss") filled the airwaves.

An overnight sensation, the radio soon became a common sight in American homes. Sales of radio sets skyrocketed by 1,400 percent from 1922 to 1929. The growth of radio introduced Americans to a cornucopia of new sounds and experiences. Want a ringside seat to a championship fight in a distant city? A prized spot on the floor of a major political convention? A seat on the reviewing stand at the Rose Bowl parade? Radio could put you right in the middle of the action. Millions of Americans who had never even heard a celebrity speak before could now recognize the voices of Babe Ruth, Clarence Darrow, Calvin Coolidge, and other luminaries, thanks to the magic of radio.

Radio also introduced millions of Americans to the beautiful sound of jazz. For many whites who had little or no contact with blacks, listening to jazz on the radio marked their first exposure to African-American music. By showcasing jazz, radio provided blacks and whites with a shared cultural experience. In so doing, it helped Americans take some of their earliest small steps toward bridging the racial divide.

The most popular proponent of the symphonic jazz sound was band leader Paul Whiteman. Throughout the '20s, Whiteman led the most popular band in the United States. Whiteman's main innovation was taking the jazz band and adding new members until it approached a symphony orchestra in size. The larger ensemble allowed Whiteman to create a hybrid version of jazz that often featured elements of show tunes and classical music.

In February 1924, Whiteman's band achieved national acclaim when it gave a concert at Aeolian Hall in New York with George Gershwin performing on the piano. One of the "secrets" to Whiteman's success was his ability to surround himself with great musical talent. Among the artists who were part of his band were Bix Beiderbecke, Jimmy and Tommy Dorsey, Hoagy Carmichael, and a young singer from Washington state named Bing Crosby.

Although his jazz wasn't as authentic as that of Louis Armstrong or Fats Waller, Whiteman helped open America's ears to new musical concepts with songs like "My Heart Stood Still" and "Oh, Lady Be Good!" This made him one of the first superstars of the broadcast age and helped usher in a new era in popular music.

WOMEN FIND A VOICE

The '20s gave voice to a new generation of American women. In the decade's first year, the Suffrage Amendment became law, empowering women with the right to vote. On the home front, new developments like canned food, ready-to-wear clothing, and electric washing machines were freeing women from many routine domestic tasks, leaving them with more time to express themselves in other areas. More women were going to college and demanding to be treated as the equals of men.

No one epitomized the new spirit of women in the '20s more flamboyantly than the flapper. The smart and sassy heroine of the Jazz Age, the flapper defied conventions of "acceptable" behavior for women. If women had traditionally worn their hair and dresses long, the flapper cut her locks short and raised her hemline to the knee. Not only did the flapper wear rouge (something her mother never would have dared do), she even applied it in public!

The flapper's rebelliousness went beyond fashion. Confident and assertive, she partook of life with the same gusto and verve as her male companions, whether this meant driving in fast roadsters or dancing the night away to a jazz band at a speakeasy.

In the world of music, female artists like Bessie Smith, Sophie Tucker, and Fanny Brice spoke to the dreams and aspirations of the Jazz Age woman. Like their flapper fans, these artists were bold and even a little brazen in their determination to overthrow traditional ideas about a woman's "proper place." Their music was infused with a passion and sensuality that would have made a Victorian maiden blush.

Smith is widely regarded as one of the greatest blues singers of all time. She made her recording debut with pianist Clarence Williams in 1923, and their record sold an amazing 750,000 copies. During the '20s, she toured and recorded with many of the leading jazz musicians including Louis Armstrong, Fletcher Henderson, and Coleman Hawkins.

Songs like "Nobody Knows You When You're Down and Out" gave Smith the opportunity to showcase the raw emotional power of her classic blues singing. Born in 1895, Smith developed her soulful style in the African-American community of Chattanooga, Tennessee, where she performed as a street singer and as a member of a vaudeville show.

Like Smith, the legendary Sophie Tucker ("The Man I Love") also got her start in vaudeville. Big, bawdy, and bursting with non-stop energy, Tucker was a gutsy performer who wasn't afraid to challenge her audience or laugh at herself. A woman ahead of her time, Tucker liked to tweak the nose of convention in her performances and challenge the traditional roles of men and women in relationships.

Fanny Brice was another great artist who mixed impulsive humor and beautiful music in the '20s. A star in *The Ziegfeld Follies*, Brice possessed a voice that was strong yet vulnerable. She could have an audience rolling with laugher one minute and then move it to tears the next with a hauntingly sweet rendition of her classic, "My Man."

A song about a woman's determination to stick with her partner regardless of circumstances, "My Man" had an especially poignant meaning for Brice. Married to Jules Arnstein, a handsome but feckless con man, Brice stuck with her husband through his numerous misadventures, serving as a pillar of strength for the couple's two children. When Brice first performed "My Man" in 1921, the song's lyrics were colored by the passions of this great lady's personal tragedies.

In today's world, when stars like Madonna, Liz Phair, and other assertive women are treated on their own terms, we can look back on the female artists of the '20s and thank them for paving the way.

A Decade of Heroes

The '20s were a decade of rapid change and big events. Such times demanded heroes of almost mythical proportions, and America delivered them in grand style. The men and women who dominated the national stage during the Jazz Age captivated the imagination in a way that few other celebrities before or since have been able to match. Many of these larger-than-life legends are as famous today as they were more than 80 years ago. In sports there were Babe Ruth, Red Grange, and Jack Dempsey. Literary giants included Ernest Hemingway, Sinclair Lewis, and F. Scott Fitzgerald. Hollywood's brightest stars were Charlie Chaplin, Buster Keaton, Rudolph Valentino, and Greta Garbo.

In the world of music, one of the '20s undisputed giants was Al Jolson. Like the artist himself, many of Jolson's hit songs such as "California Here I Come," "April Showers," and "Toot, Toot, Tootsie" are as familiar to music lovers today as they were during the Jazz Age.

With his facile rhythm and powerful voice, Jolson was able to infuse any song with a bright, cheerful mood that captivated audiences around the world. People not only liked to listen to Jolson sing, but they also enjoyed watching him perform. A natural-born entertainer, Jolson perfected the art of connecting with his audience on stage, exuding a sense of warmth and charm that made him the toast of Broadway during the '20s. Future performers as diverse as Frank Sinatra and Elvis Presley would cite Jolson as a major influence on their styles.

In 1927, Jolson entered the history books when he starred in the Warner Bros. film *The Jazz Singer,* the first "talkie" motion picture in which spoken dialogue and music were used in synchronization with the action on the film. The runaway success of *The Jazz Singer* inspired a flood of other talkie films, as movie theater owners scrambled to wire their facilities for sound, and the era of the silent movie came to an abrupt end.

For Jolson, *The Jazz Singer* was just one of many spectacular successes during the '20s. His stage presence and incredible charisma led critics of the time to describe him as "the world's greatest entertainer." When this consummate performer passed away in 1950, all the lights of Broadway were turned off as a sign of respect, an honor that has never been bestowed on a performer before or since.

While Jolson presided as the reigning superstar of the era, other future giants were achieving their first glimmer of fame in the '20s. A young clarinetist in Irving Aaronson's band named Artie Shaw was introducing white audiences to the jazz works of his idol, Louis Armstrong. In 1926, another young clarinetist, teenager Benny Goodman, made his first recording with Ben Pollack's band. Around the same time, Jimmy and Tommy Dorsey were gaining notoriety as the Dorsey Brothers in the very popular band headed by Paul Whiteman.

Although Shaw, Goodman, and the Dorseys would have to wait another decade to achieve genuine superstardom, all of them drew their first source of inspiration from the wild, wonderful, and creatively fertile times that were the '20s.

THINGS THAT FIRST APPEARED IN THE '20s

1. Crossword puzzles
2. Radio stations
3. Movies with sound (talkies)
4. Bathing-beauty contests
5. Automatic traffic lights
6. Chanel No. 5 perfume
7. Prepared baby food (Gerber)
8. Inflatable rubber beach balls
9. Aluminum foil
10. Peanut butter cups (Reese's)
11. Frozen foods (Birds Eye)
12. Insulin treatment for diabetes

MY MAN

Words by
ALBERT WILLEMETZ and JACQUES CHARLES
English Lyric by
CHANNING POLLOCK

Music by
MAURICE YVAIN

cost me a lot, but there's one thing that I've got — It's my man
Sometimes I say if I just could get a-way With my man
Sur cet-te terr, ma seul' joie, mon seul bon-heur C'est mon homme,

Cold and
He'd go
J'ai don-

wet, tired you bet; but all that I soon for-get With my man
straight sure as fate, for it nev-er is too late For a man
-né tout c'que j'ai, mon a-mour et tout mon cœur, A mon hom-me,

He's
I
Et

My Man - 3 - 1

My Man - 3 - 3

MARGIE

Words by
BENNY DAVIS

Music by
CON CONRAD and
J. RUSSELL ROBINSON

Moderato

You can talk a-bout your love af-fairs, _____ Here's one
You can pic-ture me most ev-'ry night, _____ I can't

I must tell to you; _____ All night long they sit up-
wait un-til they start: _____ Ev-'ry-thing he says just

on the stairs, _____ He holds her close and starts to coo: _____
seems all-right, _____ I want to learn that stuff by heart. _____

CHORUS

"My lit-tle Mar-gie, I'm al-ways think-ing of you Mar-gie,

WHIP-POOR-WILL

Words by
BUD DeSYLVA

Music by
JEROME KERN

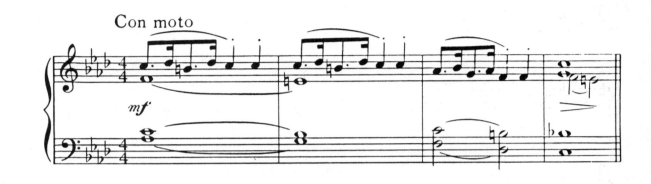

Mem-'ry takes me back a-way To an ear-ly child-hood
While the dusk-y night bird flew To the eve-ning ren-dez-

day, When I stood with-in a lit-tle wood, As day was
vous, In the dell, I've heard the ves-per bell, So soft-ly

stars were rap-id-ly fill-ing the sky.

Refrain *(gracefully)*

Whip-poor-will, I used to love to hear you call to me. Whip-poor-will,— I know he meant the world and all to me. When the sun had

gone to rest,— I could hear you from your nest,— Whip-poor-will;

You used to whis-tle ten-der-ly._____ And when the

moon would swing__ A-cross the branch-es of the trees A-

bove, You would sing__ Your plain-tive lit-tle mel-o-

CRAZY BLUES

Words and Music by
PERRY BRADFORD

Crazy Blues - 5 - 1

LIMEHOUSE BLUES

Words by
DOUGLAS FURBER

Music by
PHILIP BRAHAM

Oh! Lime - house kid___ Oh! Oh! Oh! Lime - house kid___

Go - ing the way___ that the rest of them did___ Poor brok - en blos -

- som and no - bod - y's child___ Haunt - ing and taunt - ing you're

Limehouse Blues - 2 - 1

YOU DO SOMETHING TO ME

Words and Music by
COLE PORTER

You Do Something to Me - 4 - 1

Eb Bb7 Eb espr. Ebmi. Bb7
And I gazed at you. Won't you tell me,
espr.
p
Ebmi. Eb7 Abmi. Ebmi. F7 Gmi. Gmi.7
dear, Why, when you ap - pear, Some-thing hap-pens
mf
p
Emi.7 b5 F#dim. Dmi.7 b5 C7 Fmi. B7 Bb7
poco rit
to me And the strang - est feel - ing goes through me?
poco rit
Slowly, with expression
Refrain
Eb D Eb D Eb
p-mf a tempo
You do some-thing to me.
p-mf a tempo

You Do Something to Me - 4 - 4

STAR DUST

Words by
MITCHELL PARISH
French Translation by
YVETTE BARUCH

Music by
HOAGY CARMICHAEL

Star Dust - 2 - 1

AIN'T WE GOT FUN?

Words and Music by
GUS KAHN, RAYMOND B. EGAN
and RICHARD A. WHITING

Ain't We Got Fun? - 3 - 1

CHORUS

Here's an ear full Of the chat-ter you hear:
gay and mer-ry Just at dawn-ing I heard:

Ev-'ry morn-ing, Ev-'ry eve-ning, Ain't we got fun,

Not much mon-ey, Oh! but hon-ey, Ain't we got fun. The rents un-

paid, dear,— We have-n't a car; But an-y-way, dear,—

Ain't We Got Fun? - 3 - 2

I'M JUST WILD ABOUT HARRY

Words and Music by
NOBLE SISSLE and EUBIE BLAKE

There's just one fel - low for me in this world __ Har-ry's his name __
There are some fel - lows that like all the girls, __ I mean the vamps, __

That's what I claim __ Why for ev-'ry fel - low there
With cru - el lamps, __ But my Har-ry says __ I'm the

I'm Just Wild About Harry - 3 - 1

MA!
(He's Making Eyes at Me)

Lyric by
SIDNEY CLARE

Music by
CON CONRAD

DO IT AGAIN!

Words by
B.G. DeSYLVA

Music by
GEORGE GERSHWIN

Tell me, tell me, what did you do to me? I just got a
thrill that was new to me, When your two lips were
pressed to mine. When you held me,

Do It Again - 4 - 1

LOOK FOR THE SILVER LINING

Words by B.G. DeSYLVA
Music by JEROME KERN

NOBODY KNOWS YOU WHEN YOU'RE DOWN AND OUT

Words and Music by
JIMMY COX

Key of F (C-E)

Tune Uke
G C E A

*Symbols for Guitar, Diagrams for Ukulele.

Nobody Knows You When You're Down and Out - 2 - 1

T'AIN'T NOBODY'S BIZNESS IF I DO

Words and Music by
PORTER GRAINGER and
EVERETT ROBBINS

VERSE

1. There ain't noth-in' I can do, nor noth-in' I can say,
2. Aft-er all, the way to do is do just as you please,

That folks don't crit-i-cize me;
Re-gard-less of their talk - in';

But I'm gon-na do just as I want to an-y- way,
Of-ten times the ones that talk will get down on their knees,

T'ain't Nobody's Bizness If I Do - 4 - 1

T'ain't Nobody's Bizness If I Do - 4 - 2

APRIL SHOWERS

Words by
B.G. DeSYLVA

Music by
LOUIS SILVERS

April Showers - 2 - 1

I'LL BUILD A STAIRWAY TO PARADISE

Words by B.G. DeSYLVA and ARTHUR FRANCIS

Music by GEORGE GERSHWIN

56

TEA FOR TWO

Words by
IRVING CAESAR

Music by
VINCENT YOUMANS

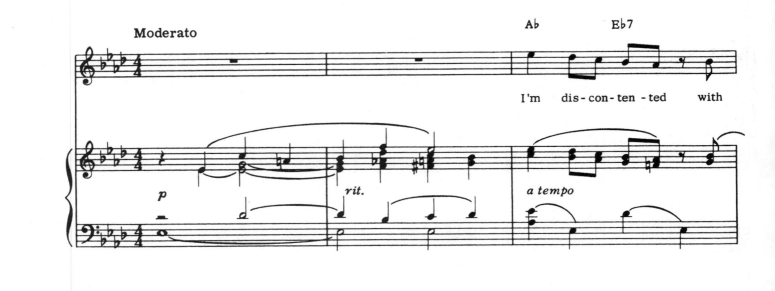

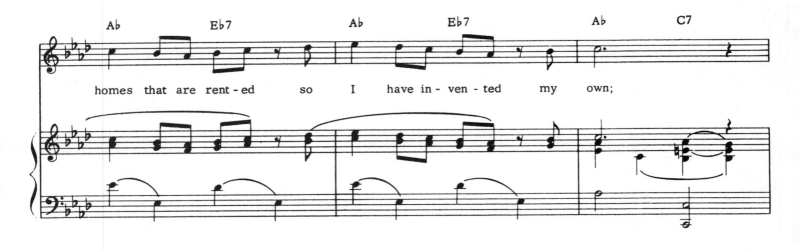

Tea for Two - 4 - 1

Tea for Two - 4 - 2

Tea for Two - 4 - 4

BUGLE CALL RAG

Words and Music by
JACK PETTIS, BILLY MEYERS
and ELMER SCHOEBEL

Bugle Call Rag - 2 - 1

63

Bugle Call Rag - 2 - 2

MORE THAN YOU KNOW

Words by
WILLIAM ROSE and EDWARD ELISCU

Music by
VINCENT YOUMANS

More Than You Know - 2 - 1

CHARLESTON

Words and Music by
CECIL MACK and JIMMY JOHNSON

Car-o - lin - a, Car-o - lin - a, At last they're got you on the map,

With a new tune, Fun-ny blue tune,

Charleston - 4 - 1

With a pe - cu - liar snap!_____ You may not be a - ble to
buck or wing, Fox-trot, two-step, or e - ven sing, If you ain't got re - li - gion,
in your feet, You can do this prance and do it neat.

REFRAIN *con spirito*

Charles-ton! Charles-ton! Made in Car-o - lin - a,__

LIZA
(All The Clouds'll Roll Away)

Words by
IRA GERSHWIN and GUS KAHN

Music by
GEORGE GERSHWIN

Liza - 4 - 1

72

Liza - 4 - 3

Liza - 4 - 4

FASCINATING RHYTHM

Music and Lyrics by
GEORGE GERSHWIN and IRA GERSHWIN

Got a lit-tle rhy-thm, A rhy-thm, a rhy-thm That pit-a-pats through my brain.

So darn per-sis-tent, The day is-n't dis-tant When it-'ll drive me in-sane.

Comes in the morn-ing With-

Fascinating Rhythm - 4 - 1

76

Fascinating Rhythm - 4 - 3

Won't you take a day off? De - cide to run a-long Some-where far a-way off, And make it

snap-py! Oh, how I long to be _ the man I used to be!

Fas-ci - nat-ing Rhy-thm, Oh, won't you stop pick-ing on me!"

me!"_____

I'LL SEE YOU IN MY DREAMS

Words by
GUS KAHN

Music by
ISHAM JONES

I'll See You in My Dreams - 2 - 2

I WANT TO BE HAPPY

Words by
IRVING CAESAR

Music by
VINCENT YOUMANS

Moderato

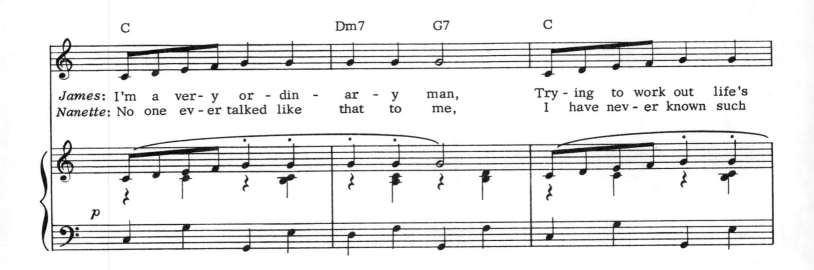

James: I'm a ver-y or-din-ar-y man, Try-ing to work out life's
Nanette: No one ev-er talked like that to me, I have nev-er known such

hap-py plan, Do-ing un-to oth-ers as I'd
sym-pa-thy, On-ly in my dreams, it real-ly

I Want to Be Happy - 4 - 1

I Want to Be Happy - 4 - 2

I Want to Be Happy - 4 - 4

THE MAN I LOVE

Music and Lyrics by
GEORGE GERSHWIN and IRA GERSHWIN

When the mel-low moon be-gins to beam, Ev-'ry night I dream a lit-tle dream,

And of course Prince Charm-ing is the theme, The he for me. Al-

The Man I Love - 4 - 1

The Man I Love - 4 - 2

SERENADE

Words by
DOROTHY DONNELLY

Music by
SIGMUND ROMBERG

Serenade - 4 - 1

O - ver-head the moon is beam - ing, White as blos-soms on the bough!

Noth-ing is heard but the song of a bird,— Fill-ing all the air with dream - ing!

Could my heart but still its beat - ing, On - ly you can tell it how! _ Be-lov-ed!

From your win-dow give me greet - ing, I swear my e - ter - nal love.

Serenade - 4 - 4

SOMEBODY LOVES ME

Words by
BALLARD MACDONALD and B.G. DeSYLVA
French version by EMELIA RENAUD

Music by
GEORGE GERSHWIN

Somebody Loves Me - 4 - 1

Somebody Loves Me - 4 - 4

WITH A SONG IN MY HEART

Words by
LORENZ HART

Music by
RICHARD RODGERS

With a Song in My Heart - 4 - 2

HARD HEARTED HANNAH

Words and Music by
JACK YELLEN, MILTON AGER,
BOB BIGELOW and CHARLES BATES

Hard Hearted Hannah - 3 - 1

102

Hard Hearted Hannah - 3 - 3

CALIFORNIA HERE I COME

Words and Music by
AL JOLSON, BUD DeSYLVA
and JOSEPH MEYERS

104

DO, DO, DO

Music and Lyrics by
GEORGE GERSHWIN and IRA GERSHWIN

Do, Do, Do - 4 - 1

SUNNY

Lyrics by OSCAR HAMMERSTEIN II
and OTTO HARBACH

Music by
JEROME KERN

Refrain (gracefully)

Never comb your hair Sun - ny! Leave the breez - es there Sun - ny! Let your stock - ing fall down, For shock - ing the town is all that you do. Smil - ing all the while

MY YIDDISHE MOMME

Words by
JACK YELLEN

Music by
LEW POLLACK and JACK YELLEN

DINAH

Words by
SAM M. LEWIS and
JOE YOUNG

Music by
HARRY AKST

Dinah - 2 - 1

If there is and you know'er, — Show'er to me? — Din - ah, — with her Dix-ie eyes

blaz-in', — — How I love to sit and gaze in - - to the eyes of Din-ah Lee. —

Ev'ry night — why do I — shake with fright, — Be-cause my Din-ah might change her mind a-bout

me. — — Din - ah, — if she wandered to Chin-a, — I would hop an o-cean

1.

2.

lin-er, — — Just to be with Din-ah Lee! — Lee! —

Dinah - 2 - 2

I'M SITTING ON TOP OF THE WORLD

Lyric by
LEWIS and YOUNG

Music by
RAY HENDERSON

121

SWEET GEORGIA BROWN

Words and Music by
BEN BERNIE, MACEO PINKARD
and KENNETH CASEY

Moderato

She just got here yes-ter-day,___
Brown-skin Gals you'll get the blues,___

Things are hot here now they say,___
Brown-skin Pals you'll sure-ly lose,___

There's ___ a big change in
And ___ there's but one ex-

Sweet Georgia Brown - 4 - 1

MOONLIGHT AND ROSES

Words and Music by
BEN BLACK, EDWIN H. LEMARE
and NEIL MORET

Refrain-Moderately *(with expression)*

Moon - light and ros - es _____ Bring won - der - ful mem-'ries of you. _____ My heart re - pos - es _____ In beau - ti - ful thoughts so true. _____

WHO?
(FROM "SUNNY")

Lyrics by
OTTO HARBACH and
OSCAR HAMMERSTEIN

Music by
JEROME KERN

Who? - 3 - 3

WHAT IS THIS THING CALLED LOVE?

Words and Music by
COLE PORTER

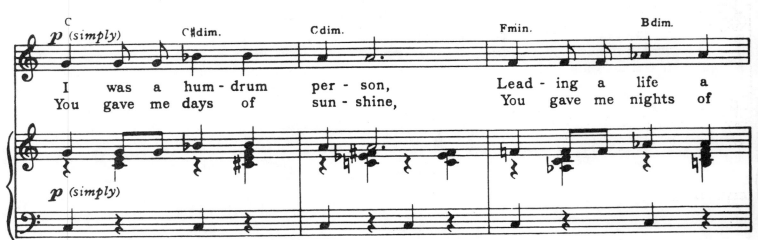

I was a hum-drum per-son, Lead-ing a life a
You gave me days of sun-shine, You gave me nights of

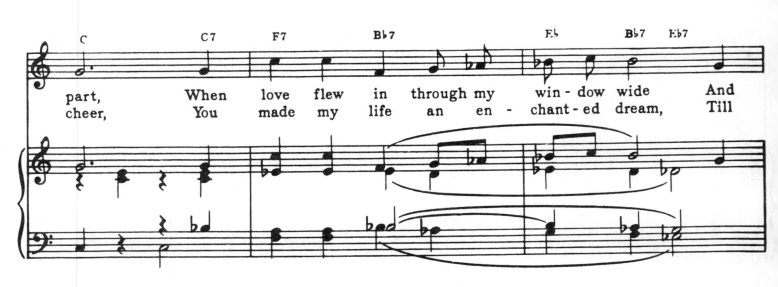

part, When love flew in through my win-dow wide And
cheer, You made my life an en-chant-ed dream, Till

What Is This Thing Called Love? - 4 - 1

134

What Is This Thing Called Love? - 4 - 4

I GUESS I'LL HAVE TO CHANGE MY PLAN

Words by
HOWARD DIETZ

Music by
ARTHUR SCHWARTZ

I Guess I'll Have to Change My Plan - 4 - 1

I KNOW THAT YOU KNOW

Words by
ANNE CALDWELL

Music by
VINCENT YOUMANS

MY HEART STOOD STILL

Words by
LORENZ HART

Music by
RICHARD RODGERS

Martin: I laughed at sweet - hearts
Sandy: Through all my school - days

I met at schools;
I hat - ed boys;

All in - dis - creet hearts
Those Ap - ril - Fool days

And then my heart stood still! ____

My feet could step and walk, My lips could move and talk,

And yet my heart stood still! ____ Though not a

sin - gle word was spok - en, I could tell you knew, ____

My Heart Stood Still - 4 - 4

MOUNTAIN GREENERY

Words by
LORENZ HART

Music by
RICHARD RODGERS

Mountain Greenery - 2 - 1

SOMEONE TO WATCH OVER ME

Music and Lyrics by
GEORGE GERSHWIN and IRA GERSHWIN

There's a say-ing old Says that love is blind, Still we're of-ten told, "Seek and
Un pro-ver-be dit l'a-mour a - veu-glé, On nous dit aus-si: "Cher-chez

ye shall find." So I'm going to seek A cer-tain lad I've had in mind.
pour trou-ver." Je cher-che ce gail-lard qui m'est res - té dans l'i - dée,

Someone to Watch Over Me - 4 - 1

Look-ing ev-'ry-where, Have-n't found him yet; He's the big af-fair I can-
Re - gar-dant par-tout sans le ren - con-trer; C'est un gars que je ne puis

not for-get. On - ly man I ev - er Think of with re - gret.
ou - bli - er. Le seul homme à qui je pense a - vec re - gret.

I'd like to add his in - i - tial to my mon-o - gram.
Mon nom pour ses i - ni - tia - les, je le chan-ge - rais.

Tell me, where is the shep-herd for this lost lamb.
Pour la bre - bis per-due, où est le ber - ger?

un poco rall.

Someone to Watch Over Me - 4 - 2

REFRAIN

There's a some-bod-y I'm long-ing to see. I hope that he Turns out to be
Il est un quel-qu'un que je veux re-voir Cha-que ma-tin et cha-que soir,

Some-one who'll watch o-ver me._____ I'm a lit-tle lamb who's
Et qui me pro-té-ge-ra._____ Je suis la bre-bis per-

lost in the wood. I know I could Al-ways be good To one who'll
due dans le bois. Je don-ne-rai Tou-te ma foi A qui me

watch o-ver me._____ Al-though he may not be the
pro-té-ge-ra._____ Quoi-qu'il ne soit pas un hom-

153

Someone to Watch Over Me - 4 - 4

IF I COULD BE WITH YOU
(One Hour Tonight)

Words and Music by
HENRY CREAMER and
JIMMY JOHNSON

* Optional verse.

If I Could Be With You - 3 - 1

THE BIRTH OF THE BLUES

Words by
B.G. DeSYLVA and LEW BROWN

Music by
RAY HENDERSON

HALLELUJAH!

Words by
LEO ROBIN and CLIFFORD GREY

Music by
VINCENT YOUMANS

How I sang a - bout the Judge-ment morn,
And of Ga - briel toot-in' on his horn.
In that sun - ny land of milk and hon - ey, I had no com-plaints,
While I thought of Saints
So I say to all who feel for - lorn:

STRIKE UP THE BAND

Music and Lyrics by
GEORGE GERSHWIN
and IRA GERSHWIN

Strike up the Band - 4 - 2

166

AIN'T SHE SWEET

Words by
JACK YELLEN

Music by
MILTON AGER

Ain't She Sweet - 2 - 1

WITHOUT A SONG

Words by
WILLIAM ROSE and EDWARD ELISCU

Music by
VINCENT YOUMANS

Slow (Andante)

With great expression but not draggy

With-out a song___ the day would nev-er end; With-out a song___ the road would nev-er bend;When things go wrong___ a man ain't

Song - 4 - 1

HE LOVES AND SHE LOVES

Music and Lyrics by
GEORGE GERSHWIN and IRA GERSHWIN

He Loves and She Loves - 4 - 1

He Loves and She Loves - 4 - 2

HOW LONG HAS THIS BEEN GOING ON?

Words by
IRA GERSHWIN

Music by
GEORGE GERSHWIN

How Long Has This Been Going On? - 4 - 1

How Long Has This Been Going On? - 4 - 4

'S WONDERFUL

Music and Lyrics by
GEORGE GERSHWIN
and IRA GERSHWIN

Moderato

He: Life has just be-gun. Jack has found his Jill,
She: Don't mind tell-ing you, In my hum-ble fash,

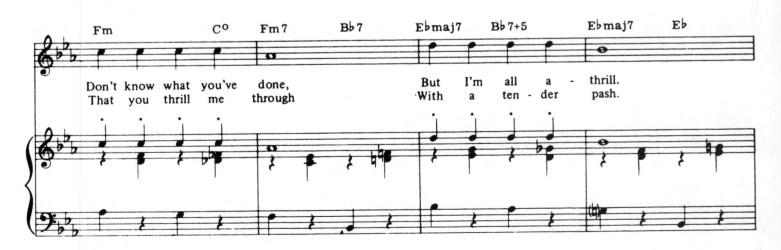

Don't know what you've done, But I'm all a-thrill.
That you thrill me through With a ten-der pash.

'S Wonderful - 4 - 1

'S Wonderful - 4 - 2

CAN'T HELP LOVIN' DAT MAN
From "Showboat"

Words by
OSCAR HAMMERSTEIN II

Music by
JEROME KERN

Fish got to swim ___ and birds got to fly, ___
Tell me he's la - zy, tell me he's slow, ___

I got to love ___ one man till I die. ___
Tell me I'm cra - zy, may - be I know. ___

Can't help lov - in' dat man ___ of

Can't Help Lovin' Dat Man - 3 - 2

THE HAWAIIAN WEDDING SONG

English Words by
AL HOFFMAN and DICK MANNING

Hawaiian Words and Music by
CHARLES E. KING

Slowly, with much warmth

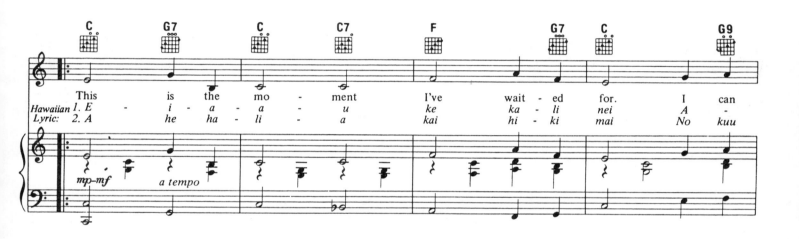

Hawaiian 1. E - i - a - a - u ke ka - li nei A -
Lyric: 2. A he ha - li - a kai hi - ki mai No kuu

This is the mo - ment I've wait - ed for. I can

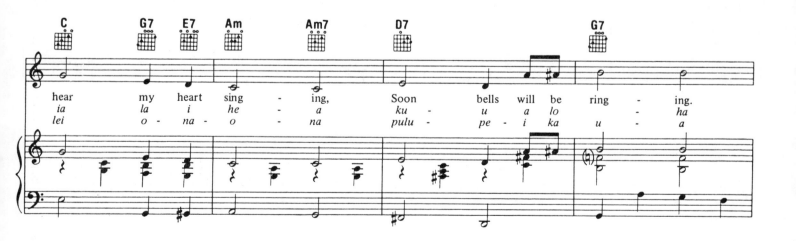

hear my heart sing - ing, Soon bells will be ring - ing.
ia la i he - a ku - u a lo - ha
lei o - na - o - na pulu - pe - i ka u - a

The Hawaiian Wedding Song - 3 - 1

The Hawaiian Wedding Song - 3 - 3

The Hawaiian Wedding Song - 3 - 3

THOU SWELL

Words by
LORENZ HART

Music by
RICHARD RODGERS

Thou Swell - 4 - 1

YOU ARE LOVE

Words by OSCAR HAMMERSTEIN II
Music by JEROME KERN

Poco agitato

Then___ my for - tune turned and I found___ you;

Here___ you are with my arms a - round___ you.

You___ will nev - er know what you've meant___ to me.

You're___ the prize that heav - en has sent___ to me.

Here's —— a bright and beau-ti-ful world —— all new Wrapped

Tempo di Valse

up —— in you. ——

Refrain (*with expression*)

You —————— are love, here in my arms

Where you be-long, And here you will stay. I'll not let you a-

ONE KISS

Words by
OSCAR HAMMERSTEIN II

Music by
SIGMUND ROMBERG

Tempo di Valse

how I don't be-lieve in the mod-ern plan,— I want to wait for just one man. One

kiss, one man to save it for,———— One love for him a-lone. One

word, one vow and noth-ing more,———— To tell him I'm his own.———— One

mag-ic night with-in his arms,———— With pas-sion flow'r un-furled,———— But

I will try to love on-ly one man And no oth-er man in the world.————

LOVER, COME BACK TO ME!

Words by
OSCAR HAMMERSTEIN II

Music by
SIGMUND ROMBERG

Moderato

mf *molto rit.*

mp a tempo

You went a-way, I let you, We broke the ties that bind; I want-ed to for-get you And leave the past be-hind. Still, the mag-ic of the night I

Lover, Come Back to Me! - 4 - 1

Love had its day, That day is past, You've gone a-way.

This ach-ing heart of mine is sing - ing: "Lov - er, come back to

me!" When I re-mem-ber ev -'ry lit - tle thing you used to do,

I'm so lone - ly, Ev -'ry road I walk a - long I've

Lover, Come Back to Me! - 4 - 4

LET'S DO IT
(Let's Fall in Love)

Words and Music by
COLE PORTER

Let's Do It - 4 - 1

WHEN YOU'RE SMILING
(The Whole World Smiles With You)

Words and Music by
MARK FISHER, JOE GOODWIN
and LARRY SHAY

When You're Smiling - 3 - 1

214

When You're Smiling - 3 - 3

TOOT, TOOT, TOOTSIE!

Words and Music by
GUS KAHN, ERNIE ERDMAN,
DAN RUSSO and TED FIORITO

AIN'T MISBEHAVIN'

Words by
ANDY RAZAF

Music by
THOMAS "FATS" WALLER
and HARRY BROOKS

BABY, WON'T YOU PLEASE COME HOME

Words and Music by
CHARLES WARFIELD and CLARENCE WILLIAMS

Baby, Won't You Please Come Home - 3 - 1

MEXICALI ROSE

Words by
HELEN STONE

Music by
JACK B. TENNEY

Mex - i - cal - i Rose, stop cry - ing;

I'll come back to you some sun - ny day.

Dm7

Ev - 'ry night you'll know that I'll be pin -

G7

ing, Ev - 'ry hour a year while I'm a -

C

way. _____ Dry those big brown

eyes and smile, dear;

OH, LADY BE GOOD!

Music and Lyrics by
GEORGE GERSHWIN
and IRA GERSHWIN

Allegretto grazioso

Lis - ten to my tale of woe, It's ter - ri - bly sad, but true.
Au - burn and bru - nette and blonde, I love 'em all, tall or small.

All dressed up, no place to go, Each ev - 'ning I'm aw - f'ly blue.
But some - how they don't grow fond, They stag - ger but nev - er fall.

I must win some win - some miss; Can't go on like this.
Win - ter's gone, and now it's Spring! Love! where is thy sting?

Oh, Lady Be Good! - 3 - 1

GET HAPPY

Words and Music by
HAROLD ARLEN and TED KOEHLER

SINGIN' IN THE RAIN

Lyric by
ARTHUR FREED

Music by
NACIO HERB BROWN

Sing— in' In The Rain, Just Sing— in' In The Rain. What a glo— ri-ous feel-ing I'm hap— py a-gain, I'm laugh— ing at clouds So

Singin' in the Rain - 3 - 1

Why am I smil-in' and why do I sing?— Why does De-cem-ber seem

sun-ny as Spring?— Why do I get up each morn-ing to start—

Hap-py and het up with joy in my heart?— Why is each new task a

tri-fle to do?— Be-cause I am liv-ing a life full of you— I'm

D.S. al Fine

Singin' in the Rain - 3 - 3

OL' MAN RIVER

Words by
OSCAR HAMMERSTEIN II

Music by
JEROME KERN

Col-ored folks work on de Mis-sis-sip-pi, Col-ored folks work while de white folks play,

Pull-in' dose boats from de dawn to sun-set, Git-tin' no rest till de judge-ment day.

Ol' Man River - 5 - 1

don't plant cot-ton, An' dem dat plants 'em is soon for-got-ten; But

ol' man riv-er, he jus' keeps roll-in' a - long.

You an' me, we sweat an' strain,

Bod - y all ach-in' an' racked wid pain. "Tote dat barge!"

Ol' Man River - 5 - 4